Michigan

BY ANN HEINRICHS

Content Adviser: Roger Rosentreter, Michigan Historical Society, Lansing, Michigan

Reading Adviser: Dr. Linda D. Labbo, Department of Reading Education, College of Education, The University of Georgia

COMPASS POINT BOOKS MINNEAPOLIS, MINNESOTA

Compass Point Books
3722 West 50th Street, #115
Minneapolis, MN 55410

Visit Compass Point Books on the Internet at *www.compasspointbooks.com*
or e-mail your request to *custserv@compasspointbooks.com*

On the cover: Miners Castle, Pictured Rocks National Lakeshore

Photographs ©: Photo Network/MacDonald Photography, cover, 1; Tom Till, 3, 8, 14, 42, 43; Unicorn
Stock Photos/ Dennis MacDonald, 5, 32; Photo Network/Jim Schwabel, 7; Unicorn Stock Photos/ Mark
Gibson, 9; Tom Walker/Visuals Unlimited, 10; Mark & Sue Werner/The Image Finders, 12; Corbis, 15;
Étienne Brûlé at the Mouth of the Humber, by F. S. Challener, 1956, Government of Ontario Art
Collection, Toronto/Thomas Moore Photography, Toronto, 16; The Newberry Library/Stock Montage,
17; North Wind Picture Archives, 18, 41; Hulton/Archive by Getty Images, 19, 20; Robert McCaw, 22,
44 (bootom left); Unicorn Stock Photos/Andre Jenny, 23, 35, 37, 47; Bruce Leighty/The Image Finders,
25; Mark E. Gibson/Visuals Unlimited, 26; Bettmann/Corbis, 27, 28; Macduff Everton/Corbis, 29; Mark
E. Gibson/The Image Finders, 31, 39, 45; Neal Preston/Corbis, 33, 46; Brian Bahr/Getty Images, 34, 48;
Photo Network/David N. Davis, 40; Robesus, Inc., 43 (state flag); One Mile Up, Inc., 43 (state seal);
Patrick Johns/Corbis, 44 (top); Gary W. Carter/Corbis, 44 (middle); Artville, 44 (bottom right).

Editors: E. Russell Primm, Emily J. Dolbear, and Catherine Neitge
Photo Researcher: Svetlana Zhurkina
Photo Selector: Linda S. Koutris
Designer: The Design Lab
Cartographer: XNR Productions, Inc.

Library of Congress Cataloging-in-Publication Data
Heinrichs, Ann.
   Michigan / by Ann Heinrichs.
       v. cm.— (This land is your land)
Includes bibliographical references (p.) and index.
Contents: Welcome to Michigan!—Forests, lakes, and shores—A trip through time—Government
by the people—Michigan at work—Getting to know Michiganians—Let's explore Michigan!—
Glossary—Did you know?—At a glance—Important dates—Want to know more?.
   ISBN 0-7565-0323-X (hardcover)
1. Michigan—Juvenile literature. [1. Michigan.] I. Title.
   F566.3 .H45 2003
   977.4—dc21   2002010059

Table of Contents

In the 1840s, a traveler named Lansing Swan called Michigan "the most beautiful country I ever saw." That beautiful country was once a vast wilderness. Its deep forests and sparkling streams were rich with wildlife. Native Americans hunted and fished there in peace. Then French fur traders began to arrive. Next came farmers, loggers, and miners.

Over time, the people of Michigan built a great state. Their lumber industry supplied the United States with wood. Tons of iron came from Michigan's mines. Copper is another mineral that comes from Michigan. Today, Michigan leads the world in making cars and cereal.

Michigan offers much more than factory goods, though. Motown music and the superstar Madonna were born in Michigan. So was the basketball star Earvin "Magic" Johnson.

Many visitors today still agree that Michigan is the most beautiful land they've ever seen. Take a look and you'll agree!

▲ Michigan is filled with great natural beauty.

Michigan is sometimes called the Peninsula State. A peninsula is a piece of land surrounded by water on three sides. Michigan is made up of two peninsulas. They are the Lower Peninsula and the Upper Peninsula. The peninsulas are connected by the Mackinac Bridge. It runs across the Straits of Mackinac.

Michigan has miles and miles of shoreline. Among the states, only Alaska's shore is longer. Michigan is the only state touching four of the five Great Lakes.

The Lower Peninsula faces Lake Michigan on the west. **Sand dunes** line this shore. On the east are Lakes Huron and Erie and part of Canada. Indiana and Ohio lie south of Michigan.

The Upper Peninsula joins Wisconsin on the west. To the north is Lake Superior. The state's highest region is the western Upper Peninsula. This land is rugged and rocky. The rest of Michigan is flat or covered with rolling hills.

Michigan's Lower Peninsula looks like a big mitten.

▲ Sleeping Bear Dunes National Lakeshore is located on Lake Michigan, one of the four Great Lakes to touch the state.

▲ This rugged rock formation is called Miners Castle. It lies along Lake Superior.

▲ Rich farmland helps make Michigan one of the country's leading producers of crops.

Its southern half has the state's best farmland. Many industrial cities are located in the south, too. Farther north, the land is hilly with lots of forests.

▲ **Moose live on Isle Royale in Lake Superior.**

Michigan's waters are dotted with many islands. The largest is Isle Royale in Lake Superior, north of the Upper Peninsula. A large herd of moose and a pack of timber wolves live there.

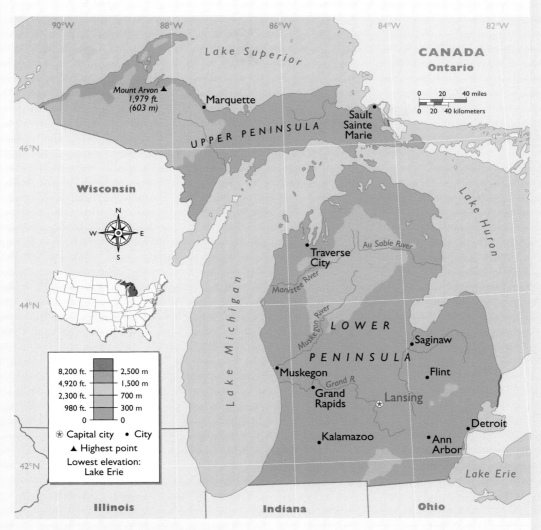

▲ **A topographic map of Michigan**

Michigan has thousands of small lakes. Many rivers and streams run through Michigan, too. Ducks and geese nest along the rivers and lakes. Rivers in the Upper Peninsula make beautiful waterfalls.

▲ Beavers build their lodges along Michigan's riverbanks.

Forests cover more than half the state and shelter lots of animals. Many deer can be found there. Beavers are found along the riverbanks. Fur traders once hunted them for their rich fur. Bears, weasels, rabbits, and raccoons also roam the forests.

Michigan's nickname is the **Wolverine** State. But why? Wolverines probably never lived there. Some people say the name was given to the state by Ohioans around 1835. This was a time when there was a piece of land called the Toledo Strip that was claimed by both states. Ohioans are said to have described the Michiganians as savage and bloodthirsty—just like wolverines. Other people say that the name came from Native Americans. They compared the settlers to wolverines because of the way the settlers took the land away from them.

Winters in Michigan are cold and snowy. The heaviest snows fall in the Upper Peninsula. Stormy winds blow across the lakes in the fall and the winter. Summertime is warm in most of Michigan, but the north never gets very hot. That's why people like to take summer vacations in the Upper Peninsula.

▲ **People living in the Upper Peninsula expect snowy winters.**

Thousands of American Indians once lived in what is now Michigan. Their dome-shaped homes were covered with bark. The women and girls farmed and cooked. They gathered nuts and berries. The men and boys hunted, fished, and made canoes.

The major Indian groups were the Odawa (Ottawa), Potawatomi, and Ojibwa (Chippewa). They joined together in the Three Fires Confederacy. The Odawa people were skilled traders. They traveled far in their birch-bark canoes.

▲ **Members of the Ojibwa tribe at the beginning of the 20th century**

    Étienne Brulé was the first European to arrive in what is now Michigan. He was a French explorer from Canada. Brulé reached the Upper Peninsula around 1620. Other Frenchmen soon followed.

    Fur traders bartered with the Indians for animal skins. Father Jacques Marquette taught Christianity to the Indians. He founded a mission at Sault Sainte Marie in 1668. This was Michigan's first permanent European settlement. Antoine de la Mothe Cadillac set up a trading center near Detroit in 1701.

▲ An Ojibwa village next to Sault Sainte Marie on the Saint Marys River

When France lost a war with Great Britain in 1763, Michigan passed to the British. Then, after the Revolutionary War (1775–1783), the land became part of the vast Northwest Territory of the United States. Michigan Territory was created in 1805. At last, in 1837, Michigan became the twenty-sixth state.

▲ Miners hoped to make their fortunes in iron mines like this one.

This new state was rich in natural resources. Loggers cut trees in its dense forests. Sawmills were built to cut the logs into lumber. The Upper Peninsula had rich deposits of copper and iron. Hundreds of miners came to seek their fortunes in the mines. Unfortunately, few actually made fortunes. New settlers also poured in to farm Michigan's rich soil.

FIRST · CAR

▲ **Henry Ford in a "horseless carriage" he built in Michigan in 1896**

The "horseless carriage" was an exciting new invention in the late 1800s. Today, we call it the automobile. Ransom Olds and Henry Ford built automobile factories in Detroit. By World War I (1914–1918) Michigan led the nation in automobile production.

▲ Workers at a Detroit factory build Dodge trucks for the army in 1942.

The Great Depression of the 1930s was hard on Michigan. People could not afford to buy Michigan's cars, and many factory workers lost their jobs. World War II (1939–1945) helped the state get back on its feet. Michigan's factories got busy making tanks, ships, airplanes, and other war materials.

Since the war, Michigan has had many ups and downs. The U.S. **economy** slowed down several times. Each time, Michigan's **industries** were badly hurt. But the hardworking people of Michigan kept bouncing back.

Today, Michigan is attracting many new industries. Tourism is booming, too. Visitors seem to believe Michigan's state motto: "If you seek a pleasant peninsula, look about you!"

Government by the People

Fifth-graders in Niles loved the painted turtle. They wanted it to be their state reptile. So they wrote to their representative in the state legislature. He told them the steps they needed to follow. They followed his instructions, and it worked! In 1995, the painted turtle became Michigan's official state reptile. These students proved that everyone can take part in government.

▲ **The painted turtle is Michigan's state reptile.**

Michigan's state government is divided into three branches—legislative, executive, and judicial. The U.S. government is set up in the same way. This system allows each branch to keep a check on the others. No single branch can become too powerful.

The legislative branch makes the state's laws. Voters elect lawmakers to serve in Michigan's legislature. The legislature has two houses, or sections—a 38-member senate and a 110-member house of representatives.

The executive branch makes sure that the state

▲ **The state capitol in Lansing**

▲ A geopolitical map of Michigan

laws are carried out. Michigan's governor heads the executive branch. Voters elect the governor to a four-year term. A governor may serve only two terms in a row. Other executive officers include the lieutenant governor and the state treasurer.

Michigan's judges and courts make up the judicial branch of the state government. Their job is to decide whether laws have been broken. Michigan's highest court is the Michigan Supreme Court. But cases begin in the state's many lower courts.

Michigan is divided into eighty-three counties. A board of commissioners governs each county. Cities elect a city council and a mayor or a city manager. Counties and cities may choose to have home rule. If they do, they can make their own charter, or set of basic laws.

▲ **The Michigan Supreme Court meets in this room in Lansing.**

To most people, "Motown" is a kind of music. They might not know that Motown is short for "Motor Town." That's a nickname for Detroit, the automobile capital of the world.

Michigan leads the nation in making cars, trucks, vans, and buses. Detroit, Dearborn, Flint, Lansing, Pontiac, and

▲ An auto transport truck carries some of the millions of cars produced in Michigan each year.

Warren are all "motor towns." Michigan's factories also make machines, metal tools, and computers. Chemical plants produce medicines, paint, and soap.

One day, Will Kellogg boiled a pot of wheat. Then he forgot it was on the stove. When he ran the wheat through some rollers, each grain of wheat became a thin, dry flake. They became crisp when baked. He tried the same thing with corn, and he got the same results. He had invented cornflakes!

Kellogg opened the Battle Creek Toasted Corn Flake Company in 1906.

▲ Will Kellogg

▲ A machine packages cornflakes in the 1950s.

Today, Battle Creek makes more cereal than anywhere else in the world. Michigan's food plants also produce canned fruits, vegetables, and baby food.

Michigan's farmers are busy, too. Southern Michigan is great for field crops. Fruits grow well along Lake Michigan. The state ranks first in the nation in the production of blueberries, cherries, and cucumbers. It's second in celery and third in apples and asparagus. Michigan is also the top state for marigolds, petunias, and flowering hanging baskets.

Only Minnesota produces more iron ore than Michigan. Oil and natural gas are found in Michigan, too. Other valuable

▲ Michigan ranks first in the nation in the production of cherries.

minerals are copper, limestone, magnesium, and gypsum.

Let's not forget Michigan's service workers. Almost four of every five workers in Michigan hold service jobs. They may be medical workers, engineers, salespeople, bankers, or teachers. They all help make Michigan a great place to live!

Getting to Know Michiganians

What do you call the people of Michigan? Some say they are Michiganians, and others say they are Michiganders. The Historical Society of Michigan has used the name *Michiganian* since 1870. But people in Michigan use whichever word they like!

Michiganians have roots in many cultures. Just look at Michigan's place names. Kalamazoo, Saginaw, and Muskegon are Native American names. French people named Detroit, Grosse Pointe, and Isle Royale. **Immigrants** from the Netherlands founded Holland. Settlers also arrived from Germany, Ireland, Finland, and Poland.

Today, about four out of five Michiganians have European **ancestors.** About one in seven residents is African-American. Asian, Hispanic, and Middle Eastern people add to Michigan's mix of **cultures.**

In 2000, there were 9,938,444 people in Michigan. That made it eighth in population among the states. About seven of every ten Michiganians live in cities or towns. Detroit is

▲ Greek Town in downtown Detroit has great restaurants and shops.

▲ Visitors enjoy the Tulip Time Festival in Holland.

Michigan's largest city. It's also the nation's tenth-largest city. The next largest are Grand Rapids, Warren, and Flint. The Upper Peninsula is very thinly populated.

Michigan's festivals are joyful, fun-filled events. Detroit presents **ethnic** festivals all summer long. Holland celebrates its Tulip Time Festival in May. In June, the German community in Frankenmuth holds a Bavarian Festival. Traverse City celebrates the National Cherry Festival every July.

Some northern towns remember their logging history with Paul Bunyan Days. Legends say that Paul Bunyan was

▲ Singer and actress Madonna is originally from Michigan.

a giant **lumberjack.** By his side was his faithful friend Babe, the blue ox.

What do Diana Ross, Stevie Wonder, and Michael Jackson have in common? They all got their start as Motown recording artists. Motown music grew out of Detroit's African-American community.

Michigan has given the world many other entertainers. They include superstar Madonna and actors Steven Seagal and Lily Tomlin. Basketball star Earvin "Magic" Johnson comes from Michigan, too.

▲ Michigan's hockey team is the Detroit Red Wings.

Michigan sports fans never have a dull moment. During baseball season, they cheer for the Detroit Tigers. Football season brings the Detroit Lions to the field. The Detroit Pistons and the Detroit Shock are the basketball teams. And the Detroit Red Wings are Michigan's hockey stars.

Football season is also the time to begin arguing. What are Michiganians arguing about? The friendly arguments are about which college football team is better—the University of Michigan Wolverines or the Michigan State Spartans!

Is it hard being a kid these days? Try going back in time at Fayette Historic Townsite on the Upper Peninsula. You'll learn about children's schools, clothes, toys, and games in the 1800s. See if you prefer their life—or decide to keep your own!

"Shanty boys" really had hard lives. This was the name given to young loggers. You'll learn more about shanty boys at Lansing's Michigan Historical Museum. While you're

▲ A sculpture called the Polaris Ring decorates Lansing's Michigan Historical Center, which houses the Michigan Historical Museum.

there, take a bumpy ride on a plank road. Pioneers built roads by laying planks of wood across muddy paths.

The Michigan State Capitol in Lansing was once the state museum. While it is no longer a museum, you can still see richly decorated offices and historic battle flags. You can also watch the state lawmakers at work.

The Gerald R. Ford Presidential Museum is in Grand Rapids. Exhibits there show you what it is like inside the White House and the Oval Office.

Be sure to explore the world's largest polar-bear exhibit at the Detroit Zoo. An underwater tunnel brings you nose-to-nose with polar bears and seals. Greenfield Village is in nearby Dearborn. There you can watch glassblowers, black-smiths, and other pioneer craft workers. Then tour the mas-sive Henry Ford Museum.

Would you climb up on a sleeping bear? You would if it were a sand dune! Sleeping Bear Dunes National Lakeshore is named for a Native American legend. A mother bear and her two cubs were swimming in Lake Michigan. The mother reached the shore, but her cubs drowned. The Great Spirit

▲ The Henry Ford Museum clock tower in Dearborn is a replica of Philadelphia's Independence Hall.

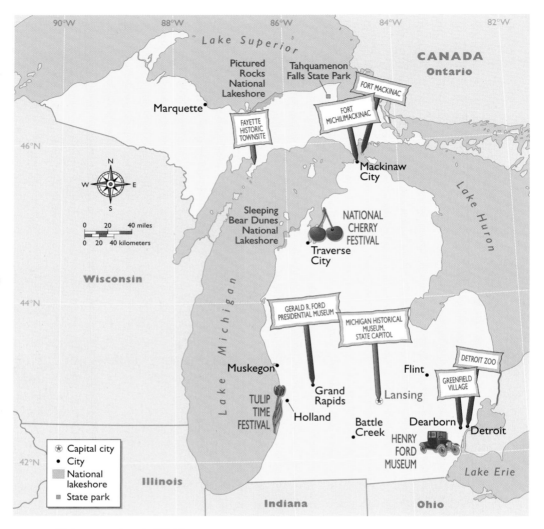

▲ **Major attractions in Michigan**

then created North Manitou Island and South Manitou Island to honor the cubs. He covered the sad mother bear with a blanket of white sand. That mound is now part of Sleeping Bear Dunes.

▲ Visitors will find only horse-drawn carriages and bicycles on the streets of Mackinac Island.

Fort Mackinac on Mackinac Island dates from the 1700s.
There you can visit soldiers' homes and dress up in antique
clothes. No cars are allowed on the island. You can ride in a

▲ Tahquamenon Falls State Park in Michigan's Upper Peninsula

horse-drawn carriage, however. Michilimackinac is a former French fort and fur-trading village in nearby Mackinaw City.

How did Michigan look to early explorers? You'll feel their sense of wonder in the Upper Peninsula. The Ojibwa fished at Tahquamenon Falls. Hiawatha, in Henry Wadsworth Longfellow's poem, built his canoe here. Bears, foxes, and other wild creatures still roam the woods. Giant colored cliffs stand at nearby Pictured Rocks National Lakeshore. You can hike for miles through the deep forests of the Porcupine Mountains. No matter where you visit, you're sure to agree—Michigan is definitely a "pleasant peninsula"!

Important Dates

1620   French explorer Étienne Brulé visits Michigan.

1668   Father Jacques Marquette establishes Michigan's first permanent European settlement at Sault Sainte Marie.

1701   Antoine de la Mothe Cadillac opens a trading post near what is now Detroit.

1763   Michigan passes from France to Great Britain.

1783   Michigan joins the United States after the Revolutionary War.

1837   Michigan becomes the twenty-sixth state.

1845   Michigan's mining industry begins.

1899   Ransom Olds opens an automobile factory in Detroit.

1903   Henry Ford opens the Ford Motor Company in Detroit.

1957   The Mackinac Bridge connects the Upper and the Lower Peninsulas.

1967   Race riots break out in Detroit.

1973   Coleman Young becomes Detroit's first African-American mayor.

1974   Gerald R. Ford becomes president of the United States.

1981   The Gerald R. Ford Library and the Presidential Museum open in Ann Arbor and Grand Rapids.

1983   Unemployment soars because of low car sales.

1992   The state capitol is restored and reopened.

2001   Detroit celebrates its 300th birthday.

Glossary

ancestors—a person's grandparents, great-grandparents, and so on

cultures—groups of people who share beliefs, customs, and a way of life

economy—the way a government runs its industry and trades goods

ethnic—relating to a nationality or culture

immigrants—people who come to another country to live

industries—businesses or trades

lumberjack—a worker who cuts down trees

sand dunes—hills of sand created by wind and water

wolverine—a fierce, flesh-eating animal

Did You Know?

★ The Chippewa gave Michigan the name *Michigama,* which means "great lake."

★ Isle Royale is home to one of the largest moose herds in the United States.

★ No matter where you are in Michigan, you are no more than 6 miles (9.7 km) from some lake or 85 miles (137 km) from one of the Great Lakes.

★ The Houghton area in the Upper Peninsula got more than 276 inches (701 cm) of snow during the winter of 1949–1950.

★ The word *peninsula* is Latin for "almost island."

★ A bridge connects Detroit with Windsor, Ontario, in Canada. This is the only spot where you travel south to get from the United States to Canada!

★ America's largest baby-food plant is in Fremont.

★ Michigan was the nation's top lumber producer from 1869 to 1900.

★ More than ninety thousand Michiganians fought on the Union side in the Civil War (1861–1865). They included white, black, and Native American soldiers.

★ Detroit was Michigan's first capital. In 1847, the capital moved to Lansing.

State capital: Lansing

State motto: *Si quaeris peninsulam amoenam, circumspice.* (Latin for "If you seek a pleasant peninsula, look about you.")

State nickname: Wolverine State

Statehood: January 26, 1837; twenty-sixth state

Area: 58,513 square miles (151,537 sq km); **rank:** twenty-third

Highest point: Mount Arvon, 1,979 feet (603 m) above sea level

Lowest point: 572 feet (174 m) above sea level along Lake Erie

Highest recorded temperature: 112°F (44°C) at Mio on July 13, 1936

Lowest recorded temperature: −51°F (−46°C) at Vanderbilt on February 9, 1934

Average January temperature: 20°F (−7°C)

Average July temperature: 69°F (21°C)

Population in 2000: 9,938,444; **rank:** eighth

Largest cities in 2000: Detroit (951,270), Grand Rapids (197,800), Warren (138,247), Flint (124,943)

Factory products: Cars and other transportation equipment, machines, metal products, chemical products, food products

Farm products: Soybeans, corn, apples, milk

Mining products: Iron ore, natural gas, oil

State flag: Michigan's state flag shows the state coat of arms on a field of blue. The coat of arms shows an American eagle holding an olive branch and arrows. The olive branch is a symbol of peace. The arrows mean that the nation is ready to defend its freedoms. Above the eagle is the nation's motto, *E Pluribus Unum*—Latin words meaning "One Out of Many." Under the eagle, an elk and a moose hold a shield showing a man on a grassy peninsula. The shield carries the motto *Tuebor*, which means "I Will Defend." It refers to Michigan's frontier days. Beneath the shield is the state motto, *Si Quaeris Peninsulam Amoenam, Circumspice,* meaning "If you seek a pleasant peninsula, look about you."

State seal: The state seal consists of the state coat of arms. Around it are the words "The Great Seal of the State of Michigan, A.D. MDCC-CXXXV." These Roman numerals stand for 1835, the date the seal was adopted.

State abbreviations: Mich. (traditional); MI (postal)

State Symbols

State bird: Robin

State flower: Apple blossom

State tree: White pine

State game mammal: White-tailed deer

State reptile: Painted turtle

State fish: Brook trout

State wildflower: Dwarf lake iris

State gem: Chlorastrolite

State stone: Petoskey stone

State soil: Kalkaska sand

Making Michigan Apple–Cherry Crumble

Apples and cherries are delicious Michigan crops!

Makes about eight servings.

INGREDIENTS:

1/2 cup flour

1/4 cup brown sugar, firmly packed

1/4 cup margarine

1/2 cup dry oatmeal

1/2 cup regular sugar

1 teaspoon cinnamon

1/2 cup dried tart cherries

1/2 cup broken pecans (if desired)

6 cups Michigan apples, peeled and sliced (Empire, Golden Delicious, Jonathan, McIntosh, or Rome Beauty apples are good to use)

DIRECTIONS:

Preheat the oven to 350°. Have an adult help you cut the apples. Combine the flour and brown sugar in a bowl. Add the margarine. Use a fork or pastry blender to cut or mash it in. Mix until it's like thick crumbs. Stir in the oatmeal. Set this bowl aside. Combine the other ingredients. Spread them in the bottom of a 2-quart baking dish. Spread the oatmeal mixture on top. Bake about 45 minutes, until the apples are soft. Serve warm. For a special treat, put ice cream on top!

State Song

"Michigan, My Michigan"

"My Michigan," with words by Giles Kavanagh and music by H. O'Reilly Clint, was declared an official state song in 1937. However, this song is not well known and "Michigan, My Michigan" is usually sung instead in patriotic programs throughout the state. Winifred Lee Brent wrote the first version in 1862. Douglas Malloch wrote new words in 1902. His version is used today.

A song to thee, fair State of mine,
Michigan, my Michigan;
But greater song than this is thine,
Michigan, my Michigan;
The whisper of the forest tree,
The thunder of the inland sea;
Unite in one grand symphony
Of Michigan, my Michigan.

I sing a State of all the best,
Michigan, my Michigan;
I sing a State with riches blest,
Michigan, my Michigan;
Thy mines unmask a hidden store,
But richer thy historic lore,
More great the love thy builders bore,
Oh, Michigan, my Michigan.

How fair the bosom of thy lakes,
Michigan, my Michigan;
What melody each river makes,
Michigan, my Michigan;
As to thy lakes the rivers tend,
Thy exiled children to thee send
Devotion that shall never end,
Oh, Michigan, my Michigan.

Thou rich in wealth that makes a State,
Michigan, my Michigan;
Thou great in things that make us great,
Michigan, my Michigan;
Our loyal voices sound thy claim
Upon the golden roll of fame
Our loyal hands shall write the name
Of Michigan, my Michigan.

Ralph Bunche (1904–1971) helped found the United Nations. He was the first African-American to win the Nobel Peace Prize (1950).

Madonna Ciccone (1958–), or simply "Madonna," is one of today's best-known singers. Madonna (pictured above left) also starred in the movies *Desperately Seeking Susan* (1985) and *Evita* (1996).

Gerald R. Ford Jr. (1913–) was the thirty-eighth president of the United States (1974–1977). He became president when Richard Nixon resigned. Ford was born in Nebraska and grew up in Grand Rapids.

Henry Ford (1863–1947) founded the Ford Motor Company in Detroit. His Model T Ford was very popular. He raised his workers' minimum wage to $5 a day—more than twice the usual rate at that time.

William Kellogg (1860–1951) invented cornflakes. He founded the Kellogg breakfast cereal company in Battle Creek.

Charles Lindbergh (1902–1974) made the first nonstop, solo airplane flight across the Atlantic Ocean in 1927.

Father Jacques Marquette (1637–1675) was a French explorer and missionary. He founded Michigan's first permanent European settlement. With Louis Jolliet, he explored the Mississippi River.

Ransom Olds (1864–1950) opened the Olds Motor Works in Detroit in 1899. It was Michigan's first automobile factory.

Pontiac (1720?–1769) was an Odawa chief. He united many tribes to fight the French and British. In Pontiac's War (1763), his warriors captured nine British forts and tried to take Detroit.

Diana Ross (1944–) was the lead singer in the Supremes, a Motown singing group. She starred as Billie Holliday in the movie *Lady Sings the Blues* (1972).

Coleman Young (1918–1997) was the first African-American mayor of Detroit. He was born in Alabama.

Want to Know More?

At the Library

Appleford, Annie, Michael Monroe, and Kathy-Jo Wargin. *M Is for Mitten: A Michigan Alphabet.* Chelsea, Mich.: Sleeping Bear Press, 1999.

Binstadt, Chari Yost, and Ken Scott. *Up North in Michigan.* Renton, Wash.: Partners Book Distributing, 2000.

Joseph, Paul. *Michigan.* Edina, Minn.: Abdo & Daughters, 1998.

Sirvaitis, Karen. *Michigan.* Minneapolis: Lerner Publications, 1994.

Wargin, Kathy-Jo, and K. L. Darnell. *The Michigan Reader: For Boys and Girls.* Chelsea, Mich.: Sleeping Bear Press, 2001.

Wargin, Kathy-Jo, and Gijsbert Van Frankenhuyzen. *The Legend of Sleeping Bear.* Chelsea, Mich.: Sleeping Bear Press, 1998.

On the Web

Michigan

http://www.michigan.gov/
To visit the state web site, with information on Michigan's history, government, economy, and land

Travel Michigan

http://www.michigan.org/
To visit Michigan's tourism web site, showing places to go and things to see

Through the Mail

Library of Michigan
717 West Allegan Street
P.O. Box 30007
Lansing, MI 48909
For information on Michigan's economy

Travel Michigan
201 North Washington Square
Lansing, MI 48913
For information on interesting places to visit

On the Road

Michigan State Capitol
Michigan and Capitol Avenues
Lansing, MI 48909
517/373-2348
To visit Michigan's state capitol

Michigan Historical Museum
717 West Allegan Street
Lansing, MI 48909
517/373-3559
To learn more about Michigan's history

Index

About the Author

Ann Heinrichs grew up in Fort Smith, Arkansas, and lives in Chicago. She is the author of more than eighty books for children and young adults on Asian, African, and U.S. history and culture. Ann has also written numerous newspaper, magazine, and encyclopedia articles. She is an award-winning martial artist, specializing in t'ai chi empty-hand and sword forms.

Ann has traveled widely throughout the United States, Africa, Asia, and the Middle East. In exploring each state for this series, she rediscovered the people, history, and resources that make this a great land, as well as the concerns we share with people around the world.